AF576237

MY LIFE VALUES II

- described in 21 Reflections and 94 Food for Thought

George Manus

Author: George Manus
Copyright: © 2024 George Manus
Design and Layout: Ole Praud

Publisher: BoD • Books on Demand GmbH, In de Tarpen 42,
22848 Norderstedt, Germany
Print: Libri Plureos GmbH, Friedensallee 273,
22763 Hamburg, Germany

You are heartily welcome to quote from this book, respecting the copyright.

George's online bookstore -
www.georgemanus-books.com

The Art of George Manus online store -
www.georgemanus.com

George's innovation & hub website -
www.maxmanusinnovation.com

George Manus e-mail: - info@georgemanus.com

ISBN: 978-87-4305-922-6

Other books written by George Manus

THOUGHTS	English
TANKER	Norwegian
REFLECTIONS I	English
REFLEKSJONER I	Norwegian
REFLECTIONS II	English
REFLEKSJONER II	Norwegian
REFLECTIONS III	English
REFLEKSJONER III	Norwegian
A WOMAN'S MANY MIGRATIONS	English
EN KVINNES MANGE FLYTTINGER	Norwegian
STORIES & THOUGHTS I	English
HISTORIER OG TANKER I	Norwegian
STORIES & THOUGHTS II	English
HISTORIER OG TANKER II	Norwegian
INNOVATIONS AND CREATIONS	English
MAX MANUS FIRMAENE - 70 år i kommunikasjon	Norwegian
WORDS FOR THE ROAD - ORD MED PÅ VEIEN I	English - Norwegian
WORDS FOR THE ROAD - ORD MED PÅ VEIEN II	English - Norwegian
WORDS FOR THE ROAD - ORD MED PÅ VEIEN III	English - Norwegian
WORDS FOR THE ROAD - ORD MED PÅ VEIEN IV	English - Norwegian
WORDS FOR THE ROAD - ORD MED PÅ VEIEN V	English - Norwegian
WORDS FOR THE ROAD - ORD MED PÅ VEIEN VI	English - Norwegian
WORDS FOR THE ROAD - ORD MED PÅ VEIEN VII	English - Norwegian
WORDS FOR THE ROAD - ORD MED PÅ VEIEN VIII	English - Norwegian
WORDS FOR THE ROAD - ORD MED PÅ VEIEN IX	English - Norwegian
WORDS FOR THE ROAD - ORD MED PÅ VEIEN X	English - Norwegian
FOOD FOR THOUGHT - 1001 Short reflections	English
TANKEVEKKERE - 1001 korte refleksjoner	Norwegian
217 REFLECTONS - Reflections on big and small	English
217 REFLEKSJONER - Refleksjoner over stort og smått	Norwegian
"THE MISCHIEVOUS BOY - and The War Hero"	English
"RAMPEGUTTEN - og Krigshelten"	Norwegian
MY LIFE VALUES I	Norwegian
MY LIFE VALUES II	Norwegian

Introduction

March 23

In this second book of two, which in no way purports to be a textbook, I have, as in the first, selected 21 Reflections from my book "217 Reflections", published in 2020. All of them are in one way or another related to "Essential Life Values and Challenges". The first was written in 1990 and the last in 2023. They were put on paper to test my opinions and thoughts on Life Values and Challenges.

The 94 Food for Thought are collected from my book: "Food for Thought - 1001 short reflections", published in 2020. They are inserted after each Reflection and related to these.

Both books are intended to give you an insight to how I look at life values and challenges.

Many of my Reflections are very personal and were never meant to be published in this way. However, they have now been put together in these two books, because of feedback I have received from people who has read both my Reflections and Food for Thought.

Honest self-awareness gives you a solid platform to stand on in life, it is a gift not given to all; many must work towards that goal themselves and this is where this book, as an example, shows you how I have exposed my honest self-awareness.

Read, digest, and take a rest.
Compare with your own thoughts and pick out the best.
Your self-awareness will thus be strengthened,

and your platform more solid and firm,
making solving life's challenges easier in turn.

Only by reading slowly and with engagement will you benefit from using this book to help you face life's challenges.

In my opinion, and based on my assumptions, I have long ago had the ideology in life, that just as surely as we are different and have our own personal identity the Creator has given us the opportunity to choose between two diametrically different forms of life, the Good and the Evil.

As I am not a fan of black/white solutions, it becomes more nuanced when I say that with extended self-awareness, we can decide for ourselves where, on the scale between the two extremes, we want to be. The choice is up us.

Fanaticism is the starting point for wrong views, so, in this context, the two extreme forms of life, either the Good or the Evil will turn out to be conflict-creating.

By reading my personal Reflections and the short Food for Thought, you will quickly understand that I would like to appear firmly rooted in the Good lifestyle.

In my eighty-fifth year, I am still working on the fine-tuning. Nothing is perfect in life.

I would be very happy if you can find inspiration in this book, for expanded thoughts which can give you better self-confidence and a more solid platform to stand on when facing life's challenges.

I recommend keeping the book on hand and using it when you are at a crossroads in life.

DEDICATION

May these books become inspiration, guidance, and reflection for **my family descendants** on their own life's journey. "My Life Values I and II" are written with love, hope and based on my experience over a long period. Find strength and joy in living according to Life Values that are important to you and yours.

THE MIDDLE WAY

The answer is always the Middle Way.
So, it was with Aristotle and so it is today.
Not too much greed and not too much spending.
Not too aggressive and not too defending.
Not too evil and not too good.
This is what I have understood.

1995

MY LIFE VALUES II

- described in 21 Reflections and 94 Food for Thought

The following is my recommendation on how to maximize the book's benefits, be it through group discussion, life coaching or as an individual reader

1. Read or discuss all the "Reflections" and note those that are most relevant to you, considering your own personal values at the same time.

2. Set aside the ones not relevant to you at the moment and concentrate on the ones that are relevant.

3. Take a good look on the associated "Food for Thought" and form an opinion about them.

4. Compare my view of the Reflection in question, with yours.

5. Form opinions on the Reflection's you have read/discussed and take a note of them.

6. Follow this procedure for each Reflection that you feel is important to you.

From this solid platform you have now created for yourself, you will have become more aware and self-confident of how to face life's challenges.

IMPORTANT INFORMATION!

Note the date below the heading of the Reflection you are reading, when it is given.

From this you will understand that my Reflections span more than 30 years, meaning that the content has been created in steps with challenges that I, like everyone else, have faced.

REGRET

2015

Most probably we all feel instinctively what it means to regret something, and it would be strange if not all of us could find personal examples related to this.

For myself, I make the matter of regret a definitive case. Either you regret something you have done, or you regret something you have said or written.

To regret something you have done, may often set big marks and give consequences which are irrevocable, while to regret something you have not done may give you, in most cases, a kind of longing, but it is normally something you can easily accept to live with.

In 1994, I wrote some words, which I think covered my attitude to this back in my business-days.

I regret very little of what I have done,
as luckily my memories quickly gone.

I regret more what I didn't get done,
all of which would have been second to none.

Gave people a chance - from near and far,
always kept the door ajar.

Yes, it has often been very dear and
hasn't always got out of low gear.

A tougher stand with demands and decision -
would that have been the answer to greater expansion?

Undoubtedly short term but wherein lies the strength,
in those who know their profession at length.

One needs practical experience and time to roost,
maturity, effort and lots of boost.

Instinctively, you know immediately that something you have said, should have preferably remained unsaid. As a rule, it is too late to regret, and consequences will follow.

I hope I have grown better as the years have passed by; in my youth I think I was more than normally big mouthed. We have all got our ways to stand out, I suppose. All the way back to those days, when I was sixteen, I still bear with me one terrible example of something I said. It can never be erased, however much I would like it to be. The episode is too grim to present here, but I only mention this because I am convinced that I am not alone having these kinds of thoughts. Also, because to regret in this way can hurt badly.

Next follow two short rhymes I put on paper many years ago, and I hope they can serve as a reminder to someone.

Gossip

The words that wander from mouth to ear -
can for some be sad to hear.
So let the thoughts in your mind go around,
before you put them to paper or sound.

To paper

When you put to paper what you think and mean -
it can be interpreted wrongly and lead to a scene.

MY FOOD FOR THOUGHT ON REGRETS

REGRET I

I Regret very little of what I have done,
as luckily my memories are quickly gone.
I Regret more what I didn't get done,
all of which could have been second to none.
2015

REGRET II

We have all done something we Regret
and which we later in life wanted to make right.
Sept. 2019

REGRET III

Instinctively, you know immediately that something you have said, should have preferably remained unsaid. As a rule, it is too late to regret, and consequences will follow.
2015

ABOUT HAVING REGRETS

You must never think that what you may eventually regret will disappear by setting a few words on paper, as a way to make up. It is not so easy, nor, of course, should it be.
However, if you are a little more conscious in your awareness every day, I believe that you can reduce your anger account and, thereby, make your life easier to live.
1994

ACCUSATIONS AND LIES

March 2014

Fairness is an important element in everyone's life - especially in early childhood and adolescence. That's because it is in this phase of your life that you become acquainted with fairness for the first time, often in connection with accusations of various kinds, both true and false.

As soon as your upbringing starts to focus on what's right and what's wrong, and that's one of the first things you are confronted with, you become acquainted with accusations.

Accusations are a completely natural occurrence in your up- bringing.

If at an early stage in your development you have a clear concept of what is right and what is wrong, you are indeed lucky, but it can hurt a lot the first time you suffer a false or wrong accusation.

If you are accused of something you have done and know deep down that you have done it and that it was wrong, other factors are brought in automatically. You must consider whether you want to admit to it or not. If you believe that the consequences of making an admission will be major it's only human to deny the accusations, as you can frequently see.

Lies are probably one of the first things you learn about in life, as early on you must test how far you can toe the line and what consequences it has when you overstep it.

Perhaps a separate reflection about the lie would be a good idea, but that'll have to wait until a more suitable occasion.

The false accusation or the incorrect one is the one which really hurts. It can, of course, be based on a lack of information, which might easily have been obtained and thus it helps create even greater misunderstanding.

Case dismissed without further consequences, but if the in- correct accusation is so one-sided and steadfast that it can't be disproved, then things might become dangerous.

I was far from an exemplary pupil. Homework was almost non-existent and if I could make mischief, for which I had a great ability, I did. Naturally enough, seen from the point of view of the teachers, it thus became very easy to blame me, even for things I hadn't done. I can't recall any serious charges, but even the few times it happened, it was extremely painful.

The sense of fairness is for most of us a strong one.

If not, how can it be possible to commit such an injustice?

So-called "justice murder", which is what a miscarriage of justice is called in Norwegian, is probably at the top of the list when it comes to incorrect accusations. (According to Wikipedia the expression miscarriage of justice is used when a person has been convicted in a court of law of a crime he or she hasn't committed.)

Originally the Norwegian expression was used when someone was wrongly convicted and sentenced to death, but as this method of punishment became less common or was finally abolished, the expression has been given an extended meaning. The strong word "murder" illustrates the criminal act which contributes to or causes an innocent person to be sentenced and detained.

Fortunately, miscarriages of justice don't happen too often, but imagine what a meaningless and desperate situation a person must be in when it does happen. I would like to include the details of a recent personal experience.

My wife's newly acquired white-painted Hyundai i30 was parked in its normal place, in front of our apartment, while we were away for a few weeks, as we had used my car to travel to the airport.

Back home again and almost immediately after we had brought our suitcases inside, the doorbell rang. The caretaker, who also keeps an eye on our apartment when we're away, informed us that, just a couple of days after we had left, he had seen a certain neighbour, back his blue-painted car, also a Hyundai but a larger model, out of the car park. By accident or poor judgement, he scraped along the side of my wife's car and left some heavy blue marks on the white paint. We had already noticed, when we parked after arriving home from the airport, that his car, which before we left had various small dents on the right side, had been newly painted and was without a scratch.

We knew that he had previously backed into one of the outside lights in the driveway and broken it, but how any new dents had been acquired was, of course, none of our business.

The following day my wife got in touch with the neighbour and in their mother tongue, which is French, she appraised him of the damage to her car.

To her consternation he denied that he had anything to do with it and pointed out that his newly painted car was without a scratch. I've seldom seen such nerve, but then he happens to be a very unpleasant person.

The neighbour in question rents the house he's living in, and I doubt that he'll ever read this, but should he happen to do so, I hope he'll understand why we now completely ignore him.

We could, of course, have taken him to court, and experienced a lot of frustration as a result, but life is too short for such things at our age.

This is one of those cases where you put up your hands and say to yourself:

"Where there is nothing, even the emperor's power ceases".

Here I don't have any material things in mind, poor man.

People of his kind probably think of themselves as winners; after all, he was spared the expense.

MY FOOD FOR THOUGHT ON ACCUSATIONS AND LIES

ACCUSATION I

If you are accused of something you have not done and you are aware that you have done it and that it was wrong, the assessment comes as to whether it is something you want to admit or not.

2014

ACCUSATIONS II

The false accusation is the one that really stings.

2014

ACCUSATIONS III

Defending that "correct" accusations be rejected cannot be recommended.

2014

ACCUSATIONS IV

If at an early stage in your development you have a clear concept of what is right and what is wrong, you are lucky,
but it can sting extra hard when you first become acquainted with a crazy or incorrect accusation.

ACCUSATION V

Accusations are one of many factors in our upbringing. When you are confronted with what is right and wrong, you become familiar with Accusations.

2014

ACCUSATIONS VI

In general, you should be careful about handing out Accusations. It is easy to forget that one of the worst things that can happen to another person is to be Accused of something they have not done.

2020

LIE I

An honest person is not strong enough to carry a Lie.

2018

LIE II

In my opinion, one of society's biggest Lies, which most of us in the so-called modern world have grown up with, is that we are all equal. Humans never have and never will be equal.

2019

CONSCIOUSNESS – UNCONSCIOUSNESS

December 2014

The shortest explanation I can get out of Wikipedia related to this contradiction goes as follows: "Only those with a functioning brain have consciousness, while unconsciousness is a common term for psychological processes a person is not aware of. To be conscious or unconscious is an either or. Either you are conscious or unconscious in a situation or action".

However, this cannot be seen to resemble Shakespeare's: "To be or not to be".

I can very well see that with these two extremes, either or, it becomes rather narrow. In between lies a sea of nuances.

Nevertheless, in this case, I prefer to make it simple: conscious, or unconscious. This way it's much easier to understand.

Let me at once make clear that at times - although I hope not too often -, I surely function as if I am unconscious.

I believe that I am normally quite conscious in my daily life.

My interpretation of that is that, among other things, it has to do with paying attention to the fact that I am not the only person on this earth or, more realistically, that normally you aren't the only person present where you happen to be.

Not one day passes without me seeing people acting

unconsciously.

The reason for putting this reflection down on paper has its background in an experience I had during our recent visit to Copenhagen.

December, board meeting, but also as usual a visit to the famous Tivoli. Fantastic Christmas atmosphere everywhere. In this context Copenhagen, can be recommended as a wonderful place to spend some days at this time of the year.

The traditional walk down Strøget, the famous pedestrian street stretching a little more than one kilometre, is always an experience, particularly at that time of the year when decorated for Christmas

We arrived from what I call the top, being the Town Hall and ambled down Strøget.

As my wife and I have been there almost every year since we married in 1998, we feel at home there.

A variety of entertainers do their best to make people stop, have a look, and maybe leave some coins before they carry on.

Strøget, as the stretch is called, starts at the Town Hall and it's first part is called Vesterbrogade. That turns into Nygade which then continues to Vimmelskaftet. After that comes Amagertorget, which brings you to Østergade. That ends at Kongens Nytorv being only a stone's throw from the famous Nyhavn. With a row of characteristic small restaurants along the canal, the place is an experience.

Just having arrived at Østergade and without it being

any tribulation I, suddenly felt an "axe hew" to my right heel.

I scream out and sink into my knees.

Of course, it's not about an axe, but the hit was perfect centred on the Achilles' heel.

When I managed to turn myself, I saw two young men behind me, one with a trolley full of newspaper, more than a meter high, and the other with an umbrella and a little folder under his arm.

Both apologised and behaved in an exemplary manner, whereby I found no reason to adopt a sombre voice.

I uttered a comment that things seem to be all right and limped along, fully aware that what could have happened did not.

Earlier I had previously had a real accident with the Achilles heel, so I know from experience what that means.

That previous occasion was my own fault and happened on a tennis court.

In his state of total unconsciousness, the master of the trolley was most probably engrossed in a discussion with his friend, the one with the umbrella and the folder.

Maybe you will give him a milder verdict than him being unconscious, for instance that he only was inattentive.

MY FOOD FOR THOUGHT ON CONSCIOUS - UNCONSCIOUSNESS

AWARENESS

Acting with Awareness in daily life you will avoid many challenges, while helping others not to get into trouble.

Sept. 219

CONSCIOUS - UNCONSCIOUS II

If you master Consciousness, Unconsciousness will have little leeway. But be careful

2023

CONSCIOUS – UNCONSCIOUS III

In the Unconscious state, you are not able to act Consciously - you are fully Conscious but acts Unconsciously.

2019

CONSCIOUS – UNCONSCIOUS IV

All Conscious people are able to register the extent to which Unconsciousness is widespread.

2019

DETAILS

2017

In many ways it's a pity that details matter, as they are mostly boring and time-consuming to get in place. I once wrote this about details in 2015.

"Many details are boring; but not all. For me, it's like details are often boring; but if it's about a detail needed to solve a challenge, I can be completely concerned about finding that detail, big or small."

Nevertheless, generally I am convinced that details matter, and that they are often boring.

I have dealt with "The Bagatelle". That reflection was written in April 1994 and starts as follows: "I'm a tiny bagatelle, a word, a smell, a taste. Spoken, felt or sensed, I can be a deciding factor in many contexts and of the greatest importance".

In the same way I believe it's often detailing that matter, and that is crucial.

It's often said that it's the small things that matter, here I am again, the bagatelle.

Doesn't it feel like a bagatelle is something small - a big bagatelle doesn't sound right, does it?

One of various definitions of a bagatelle is: "A small and less important case".

On the contrary, as I see it, a detail can be both small and big.

Anyway, maybe the detail is most often seen in conjunction with something small: "The only thing missing is the little detail".

To me this is more a matter of platitudes.

One of various definitions of a detail is: "Simplicity, part of a whole".

Well, "simplicity" has nothing to do with size and neither has "a part of a whole".

According to this, a detail gets more dimension, doesn't it?

A detailed report is by no means a bagatelle, just as details in an account are not.

Detailed descriptions of any kind one can only characterise as the opposite of having anything to do with a bagatelle.

If you look at examples like these, the "detail" and "the bagatelle" should not be used interchangeably.

Why on earth did I dig into these details, when I can clearly see the dimensions, they can occupy?

I was taught about details in a non-academic way.

During my time training with Olivetti in northern Italy as a 17-18-year-old, I was taught to be a technical instructor. After my education, I was to teach our technicians, or mechanics as they were called in those days. At the end of the fifties everything technical was still mechanical.

Without going into too much detail, what is the difference between a technician and a mechanic?

According to Wikipedia, a technician is the professional title of a person with technical working tasks; while a mechanic is a craftsman using tools to repair machines.

As, among other things, a general agent for Olivetti office machines, our company Max Manus Kontormaskiner in Norway with its branches employed about 40 mechanics at the time and had a dealer network with as many again.

In those days, a spade was called a spade.

No form of discrimination, but today I have the impression that all in this group are engineers, regardless of education, so in this context the details are probably not so important.

When it came to repairing Olivetti Divisumma 24 calculators with thousands of mechanical parts and more than a hundred adjustments of less than a millimetre, the details were of utmost importance.

Just one little wrong adjustment could be enough for the machine to fail after a repair, which means that that little detail could lead to the whole job being done over again.

Before I wrote this reflection, I googled "Olivetti calculators", hoping to find the exact number of parts the Divisumma 24 calculator consisted of, but I didn't find it.

As mentioned, many times in writing, I am hopeless when it comes to data. I'm not part of any social media and, as you can understand, I'm barely capable of navigating on google.

What strikes me, however, is that when I hit "enter" after having googled "Olivetti calculators", the first thing I see is a presentation of my book "70 years in communication" – about the Max Manus Companies from 1946 to 2016. (Norwegian edition, as it has not been published in

English).

Of course, I understand that the Danish editor BoD (Bod. dk) are doing their marketing, but that googling "Olivetti calculators" should lead to my book is, in my opinion, quite clever.

I never got hold of the exact number of parts in the Divisumma 24, but that detail – even if it is a matter of a few thousand – is presumably not important for those who have cared to read this reflection about details.

MY FOOD FOR THOUGHT ON DETAILS

DETAILS
In many ways, it's a pity that what matters are the Details, as they are often boring and time consuming to put into place.

DETAILS AND WHOLENESS
Too many Details are boring - while Wholeness is simpler.

DETAILS I
Detailed knowledge is not always necessary to make good decisions.
July 2023

DETAILS II
You can be knowledgeable without detailed knowledge.
July 2023

BREATHING EXERCISES

May 2023

Let me immediately make something clear: I have never looked for any information about the importance of breathing.

Why? Because for me it has always been something that happens by itself, something the body takes care of, something we all know must go on all the time to keep us alive.

Pretty smart. Oxygen goes into the lungs when breathing in, the blood absorbs it and transport it to all parts of the body by means of the heart that functions as a pump.

Breathe in through the nose and out through the mouth.

I believe that most of us can understand that bad blood circulation can be unpleasant and dangerous, especially if the brain doesn't get enough of it.

As a person in my mid-eighties, I have been through quite some challenges health-wise, some more serious than others; but I still wake up in the morning appreciating that I can move around, practice my hobbies and live what I call a normal life.

My blood pressure has been kept under control for the last 20 years by pills, a serious cancer operation ten years ago seems to have gone well, and a tumour in my head has had a limited increase in the last many years. Just recently it was under observation, after which the decision was taken not to operate, but to continue keeping it under observation.

As my Swiss wife had a stroke five years ago, I had to give up golf, and in the autumn of 2019, I started painting in addition to my main hobby, writing.

Like everyone else, we went through the Covid pandemic. We did not suffer personally until December 2022. After three vaccinations we then both got it, but fortunately without any nasty effects.

I forgot to mention that during some tests before my cancer operation ten years ago, my blood pressure was frequently taken, and at the same time a clip was placed on the tip of my index finger. I never thought about it but understood that it was to measure the oxygen in the blood.

Even I understand the importance of that. A low volume of oxygen taken up by the blood means less food for the various organs – very simple but still so important.

As my wife is on various medications for her stroke and must control her blood pressure every morning, loyal as I am, I made it a custom to do the same, and like her I keep a record of the results.

Everything is working well for both my wife and me.

Without going into more detail, but for reasons of curiosity, about three years ago, while not sleeping too well, I started thinking about blood and its need for oxygen to keep the organs in shape.

As my nature as an adolescent was to have my own experiences, rather than read my way through others' experiences and then to try to follow them, I started to remember some of my earlier experiences of sports, particularly clay pigeon shooting. I remember I joined a course in those days, I think it was called autogenic training. To cut a long story short: during that period when I was awake for many hours every night, I lay on my back and did as the instructor had told me, trying to relax, keeping a natural breathing rhythm. Once I had the feeling of being relaxed, I focused on the legs becoming heavy, one after the other. Then followed the arms, also making them heavy one by one. When totally relaxed with heavy legs and arms the time came to relax the muscles in the face. Then came a time to lift my arms one by one, by letting my thoughts demand that they do so. To my astonishment I could raise my arm without feeling that I had used my muscles. I could stop it at any time, and then continue the movement just with my thoughts demanding it.

Well, this was in short meant to help you relax and control your nerves. I never got to understand the part about the nerves, but I certainly have enjoyed the relaxing part many times in my life.

Going back to my curiosity, the following happened about three years ago. I suppose it was triggered by the fact that many Covid sufferers ended up with breathing problems, and that one of my worst fears is to be denied a free, unproblematic breathing.

Having finished one of the above-mentioned exercises, after having relaxed the muscles in my face, instead of lifting my arms, I started taking a deep breath. First filling the lower part of the body with air and, in the same intake, the upper part.

Keeping the air for as many seconds as possible without

feeling uncomfortable, I then slowly let the air out. While letting the air out I focused on the "imaginary train" transporting the blood to the various organs, in this case the legs.

I kept on repeating these some ten fifteen times, firstly focusing on my legs, one by one, each being a "train station" for unloading oxygen-filled blood, and then my head, in the same way. Each time trying to blow out as much as possible to make place for fresh air in the next intake.

This not only helped me to fall asleep again, but after having practised the above since the beginning of the Covid pandemic, my heart rate has established itself at a slower pace than before, and last time I went to have a massage session for my golf back, I showed the masseur my heart rate records from February to the end of April, from when I had started playing golf again, whereupon he uttered.
"You have a heart rate like mine". He is a fit under middle-aged sporty man running marathons with an average heart rate of 50 to 55.

If you want to test my way to lower your heart rate, I recommend you skip the first part about making the legs and arms heavy and relaxing the muscles in the face. Just relax some minutes in the way most suitable for you, and then start the breathing exercise.

MY FOOD FOR THOUGHT ON BREATHING EXERCISES

INNER SPIRIT

The way you look at beauty is reflected by your inner Spirit.

INNER PEACE

With Inner Peace it's easy to forward a bit of the feeling.

January 2019

INNER FLAME

If you keep your Inner Flame in a cage, you remain angry.

June 2019

STRENGTH

When we talk about Strength, we think about steel - but it can also appear like the softest eel.
When heated, things take on a different form and thus make changes to the current norm.

CONCENTRATION AND FOCUS

March 2013

Concentration is an ability which I need to improve. How can someone be capable of claiming such a thing? How can someone say for sure that they have the capability to concentrate or, as in my case, that I need to improve my ability to concentrate.

How can it be measured?

Concentration means to be so involved in something that everything else disappears.

Now I must concentrate on getting on with this reflection. In other words, I must focus on the task, get so involved in it, that everything else disappears. How do I do that? Is it like looking down into a funnel where you suddenly see everything quite clearly at the bottom; eureka?

Is there a connection between concentrating and focusing?

A lot of questions with answers few and far between.

If there's something you can't do at any given time, it's easy to blame your lack of concentration.

In the world of sports, the terms concentration and focus are well known.

Nobody wins if their concentration is absent, and they lose the ability to focus on the task at hand.

This is especially obvious in the types of sports which stretch over time, but where there is a constant need for precision performance.

As in many other contexts, golf comes to mind here.

In a space of about four hours, which is what a round

of golf should take, you must perform as few strokes as possible. All of them can be different and there are up to 14 different clubs to choose from.

Around 70 strokes and below per round, applies only to the very best players, while just over a hundred is the more normal number.

Each stroke requires full concentration and focus and the least disturbance, whether it be from the players themselves or in the form of unwanted thoughts and movements.

Any external influences can have dramatic consequences.

Regardless of the type of sport, it's often the ability to concentrate and focus that determines the winner.

Here is a typical example of my own lack of the ability to ignore external disturbances in a sporting context.

Before I got into golf, I was an active clay pigeon shooter for many years, specifically in the area called skeet.

I'll never forget the episode in which, during a championship's competition over 100 clays, I had fought my way through 99 hits and was ready for clay number 100. There was no lack of spectators, but not a sound to be heard.

One more hit would lead to a new Norwegian record for 100 clays, so with my nerves totally on edge, I got ready for the last clay. Just as I called for the clay, which is thrown from a machine in a tower at an acoustic signal from my voice, I heard a voice say loud and clear: "Now he'll become Norwegian Champion".

The shot went off the moment I got a glimpse of the clay. That was it. The amazing thing was that the person making the statement was the reigning champion.

The result was thus equal to the old record which was, of course, a big disappointment for me. It's quite possible that I would have missed anyway, but, once again, at moments like this, the deciding factor is the ability to concentrate and focus.

Apart from a Norwegian Championship gold, silver, and bronze medal in team shooting, I personally never reached a top position in the individual Norwegian Championships. My best achievement was a bronze medal in August 84 in the open Norwegian Championship.

Up until the last 25 clays, I was often well placed for top positions. The skill was obviously there, but the lack of my ability to concentrate, focus and control my competition nerves right to the end will have to take the blame.

My practise rounds were at times equal to the international top ones in those days. The best practice round ever was 197 out of 200.

For your information, in my days, normal skeet competitions lasted for two days, on which 100 clays were shot each day, so there were many waiting periods and distractions. Today, as far as I know, the rules have changed.

It's far easier for me to concentrate when it comes to finding solutions to technical challenges.

Then it's easier to suppress other disturbing factors.

But then you are immersed in yourself – not exposed like

during a competitive sport.

It is said that you can train your ability to concentrate. This I don't doubt. What I question, however, whether it's just as easy to get your competition nerves under control.

It is quite clear that some people have better control over their nerves than others, and I also have no doubt that there are those who have a far better ability to concentrate and focus than others.

MY FOOD FOR THOUGHT ON CONCENTRATION AND FOCUSING

FOCUSING

Whatever happens around you - Focus on what you stand for with humility but stick to your principles as otherwise you will lose focus.

July 2019

FOCUS AND VISION

Focusing on the goal is the most important of all - while Vision is needed to check that all conditions are in place to reach it.

CONCENTRATION AND FOCUSING I

When there is something you cannot achieve, it is easy to blame it on a lack of concentration and focus.

2013

CONCENTRATION AND FOCUSING II

There is no doubt that some people have better control over their nerves than others. Those who daily depend on being top equipped in this context will work on that matter, while the rest of us can use the time for other, for us, more important tasks.

2023

CONSEQUENCES

March 2014

The word consequence says very little. The word can be used in many contexts, one of them being to bear the consequences of your actions.

In my speech at the confirmation of my grandson, Nicolas, in September 2013, I touched on the theme consequences and that there are, for me, three stages of consequences, related to our actions, all of which count in the development of human beings.

I quote some excerpts from the speech given on the 7th of August 2013:

First there is unconscious consequence.

That's the one all children instinctively use in their development. How far can I toe the line before I overstep it, and before there are unpleasant consequences? You have throughout the years been a very frequent user of this method, Nicolas, and it seems at times, that you cross the line with the clear idea that it'll be exciting for you to see what will happen next.

This procedure is, as I've said, used by all children and is a healthy one, although it might at times be a trial for the parents.

The next one is conscious consequence.

All actions have consequences in one form or other. As time goes by you learn, however, what the consequences of your actions will be, though you often go ahead anyway. You obviously learn from it, even though it at times can result in a black eye or maybe worse. You also learn that consequences are not always the same each time even though there is the same sort of action. So, this may result in new and surprising experiences. It takes time to learn from this, something which can also be costly.

If you don't act at all, you'd think you got away with it, but then you're lagging behind in terms of experience and that can easily delay the process. To find some middle way would be my advice in this case.

The third one is a governing consequence.

That's the one where, before acting, you carefully consider the consequences.

The action doesn't take place until you have a clear idea of its consequences.

When you have reached this stage, you decide whether the action is worth its consequences and is thus well equipped for your ongoing journey through life.

You easily become confused if you look more closely at what is really meant by the word consequence.

One encyclopaedia defines consequence as a logical follow up to a prior action. This can be a fact arrived at empirically or logically, or an event-related reason for it to happen. One action may easily have several consequences.

Take a closer look at this explanation of a consequence and see if it becomes clear to you; I am having a bit of a problem with it.

Enough said, Nicolas at least seemed to think that he had understood its meaning. I can't imagine that he paid attention to the empirical or logical aspects of it; the word consequence is just something you understand intuitively, even at an early age.

The word empirical comes from the Greek "empiri", which in turn means "experience related". Not that I think you didn't already know it, but I looked it up just in case. As for the logical part, there's no need for further comment.

As for Nicolas, I believe he has a strong "empirical" reason for his understanding of consequences.

One of the consequences of having a big mouth might be that you get hit on the head. No reason to conceal that this has happened to me a few times, but it was in my early adolescence, long before I had a clear idea about consequences.

The older you get, the more experience and the better equipped you are to analyse the consequences of your actions; but you will probably never manage to avoid all the bad ones. Neither do you necessarily wish to avoid all consequences, as there are also positive ones from time to time, which you want to experience.

Oh yes, there are good consequences lying in wait all the time, even though the word consequence is used most often in unhappy circumstances.

An example of a good consequence might be that you have done a favour for someone, which has been significant for the person concerned.

The consequence then is that you get a good feeling, which is often worth much more than any other type of reward.

If you think about it, there are many actions in your everyday life which can lead to good consequences, not least among people who are close to one another. A little attention, which often costs nothing, can result in incredibly good consequences. But be aware, an unintentional word at the wrong time can lead to unintentional consequences.

At the end of last year, my wife and I undertook an action which was to have significant consequences.

I grew up with dogs and always had, up until I married my present wife, at least one English setter. As a consequence of this, I believe in all modesty to possess a certain amount of experience when it comes to dogs. My wife had a short-haired dachshund for many years before we met each other, more than twenty years ago, so she also knows what it means to have a dog. Anyway, as a consequence of acquiring her last dog – fully grown –, after a divorce had prevented the previous owner from keeping it, it was both housebroken and well behaved, so she had no experience with puppies. And to make everything clear, I must also add that it had been more than twenty years since I had had my last English setter.

On my wife's initiative, after having talked it over for some time, weighing the pros and cons, we decided in late autumn last year to check into the possibility of acquiring a little short-haired dachshund. I should add that dog number two during my first marriage was a compromise. As it wasn't too easy to have a hunting dog in a flat, we decided on a rough-haired dachshund. I wasn't going to use it for hunting purposes, as I only shot birds during my hunting days.

Because of having ordered it, the day came when the owner of the local pet shop in Vera, our nearest town, informed us that our short-haired dachshund "Duke", as it was already called by the breeder, was on its way from Toledo.

Since at that point in time we happened to be in Portugal playing golf, he consequently offered to keep it at his place for the week it would take us to get back.

All was well, and the day of the big event came, when we went to pick up our new, four-month-old family member.

The pet shop owner already had a French bulldog about four years old and, when we met the two at the shop, it was clear that little Duke had already gained some respect. The owner told us that, from the very first day, the little puppy had made it clear who got to eat first. The consequence of Duke's behaviour was that the French bulldog had immediately accepted the situation.

At the same time as we picked up Duke, my wife bought a lot of necessary equipment, such as a transport crate for travels complete with blanket, a bed to be placed in our little office, where we had decided the dog would sleep, a collar, a dog leash, fastening devices for car transport and some nappy-like rugs for the liquid and more solid stuff, which forms a natural part of everyday life. Furthermore, there was food, treats and some toys for encouragement, with and without a built-in squeaky noise. The excitement was great, and Duke passed water from pure pleasure every time we tried to pick him up.

The car had been equipped with a colourful plaid blanket, which we'd bought in Scotland earlier in the year, and which we thought would be good for him to get used to in the car.

Back home in the flat Duke immediately settled in.

Another Scottish blanket was put on one of the sofas, the one my wife normally uses, as we thought that's where the dog should stay when all three of us were at home and he felt the need to rest.

A couple of the nappy-like blankets were placed on the floor, while our new family member inspected each centimetre of the office, passageway, and the open kitchen section of the sitting room as well as the sitting room itself.

Because of his short legs, he couldn't get onto the sofa on his own, so each time he tried to do this, he was lifted. No sooner was he up there, however, before he jumped down again and disappeared into the office, immediately returning with one of his toys in his mouth. And so it went, non-stop, until he was completely exhausted. Finally, he was sleeping like a baby until a short time later he was going full speed again.

On his travels he was sometimes out of our sight and as

a consequence of our not being able to see him, he took the opportunity to do his business.

The rugs meant for this purpose were, of course, bone dry.

To make a long story short, all that was left to do was to put him in his bed in the office, turn out the light and shut the door.

As it was clear that Duke was my wife's dog, as we all know there can only be one boss, she was the one to carry out the procedure. The big question, of course, was how he would react to it.

To our great surprise, no sound was heard from him until well after seven the next morning. Then, however, there was a lot of activity going on in the office.

We heard whining and tiny whimpers, and claws scratching the door. It turned out that it was not the door to the passage and freedom that was being attacked, but the cupboard door hiding the dry dog food.

We had closely followed the instructions for meting out meals, but already after just a few days of him showing constant hunger, the consequence was a slight upward adjustment of the food quantities.

The same ritual took place each morning. My wife in slippers and housecoat, collar, and plastic bag at the ready, following behind a tail-wagging Duke, hoping that he would do his business outside. Unfortunately, a hope was usually all it was, in which case it didn't take many minutes from the time they got back in until he proudly showed us how clever he was, but seldom on the intended rugs.

We had at first decided to keep the door leading to our bathroom and bedroom shut. Everything inside there was to be out of bounds for Duke. After a bit of back and forth, using both index finger and a stern voice, it was also OK to leave the door open, so long as he could see one of us inside; but as soon as we went from the passageway into the bathroom or bedroom, it naturally became too much. Seconds later he was on his way in. The consequence being that the door remained closed most of the time. There are limits to what one can expect from a puppy, after all.

The greatest consequence of all in this case came after four weeks of having the most beautiful little puppy in the world. Practical experience and common sense told us that we were simply too "mature" to deal with the consequences resulting from having to raise a new family member and changing the lifestyle we had become used to after fifteen years.

My wife brought the matter up with the owner of the pet shop one day when she was passing by. He told her that both his wife and daughter had been very sad when they had had to give Duke away after the week he'd been there, but for obvious reason they had said nothing about it to us. He said they had already become very fond of him.

As a consequence of this, my wife asked him if he would consider taking over the responsibility for Duke. He straight away consulted his family, who immediately and with great enthusiasm looked forward to the new addition to their family.

When I say that everyone was looking forward to it, I can't vouch for the French member of the family but have since been told that they live together beautifully.

The somewhat sad consequence for us now is the loss of Duke after the four weeks we had together.

The positive consequence is that we can visit him whenever we like, and we experience the joy of seeing that he not only has a good home but also another dog as a friend – even if it is a Frenchman who has quite clearly learnt to live with the consequences of having acquired a little brother.

Did you notice the great number of times I used the word consequences in this story? How many do you think there are? You guessed right, the word is mentioned fifty-two times.

So, as you can see, there is hardly a thing which, in some form or other, doesn't have consequences. I could easily have troubled the reader with more, but then this reflection would probably have had even more unintended consequences.

MY FOOD FOR THOUGHT ON CONSEQUENCES

CONSEQUENCES I

Examples of three stages of Consequences, all of which count in the development of human beings:
The unconscious consequences - The conscious consequences and the governing consequences.

CONSEQUENCES II

The Consequences of giving someone the little finger can be fateful if you don't know them.

Nov. 2019

CONSEQUENCES - INCONSISTENCIES

Everything you do can have big or small Consequences.
Inconsistencies or lack of Consequences are achieved when you are inactive.

CONSEQUENCES - DEVELOPMENT

That children toe the line as far as they can before they experience Consequences is part of their Development.
How is it that the adults constantly continue to ignore them?
Do they never learn?

Sept. 2019

CURIOSITY

March 2013

"I wonder what I will get to see, beyond the lofty mountains". I'm not quite certain who wrote this, but I believe that it was the famous Norwegian writer Bjørnstjerne Bjørnson.

In my opinion it symbolizes curiosity. "The eye will surely meet nothing but snow".

Supposition, nothing certain, what else, curiosity.

Was it a quote from Bjørnson or someone else? Am I not curious about that?

Not really, I probably don't have the capacity to be curious about everything; that would be too time-consuming. There must be priorities.

For the sake of this reflection, I had to check it anyway and, sure enough, it was Bjørnson. "Around and about there are nothing but trees, I would very much like to get across; when will I ever dare?"

You would think after this that everyone has certain subjects for their curiosity.

If there is some truth in any of this, we're all curious, but for most of us our curiosity is limited to that which we feel strongly about or are especially interested in. In other words, the interesting question is not whether we are curious or not, as everyone is curious to some extent or other.

Does this mean that if you don't have the ability to ask questions, or are indifferent to finding answers to your questions, or if you haven't got any questions at all, then you are lacking in curiosity?

Probably yes; but again, most people find ways of showing their curiosity within their areas of interest, and thus find answers to their questions.

There's nothing wrong in that, as we don't all have to be the same. In my case, curiosity is the same as being and feeling alive.

I see it as a driving force, that which makes you put one foot in front of the other in your everyday life.

Curiosity is the driving force behind progress.

Forget the curiosity which makes you poke your nose into other people's business, as that seldom leads to anything good, and you're better off without such information.

It's the curiosity which asks questions beginning with "why?" which, in my mind, is the important one.

Again, when you don't ask questions, you remain single-minded, you come to a halt and don't get any further. It's good that I've concluded that we all have degrees of curiosity.

In November 1994 I wrote the reflection "Why?".

When I refer to events during my time at school in Italy as a 17–18-year-old, I wasn't as aware of things as I became later in life. That's why I asked questions like: "What makes us ask the question "Why?" so often. Is it because we're curious or because we're ignorant?"

Back then, I saw "why?" from a completely different angle to the one I saw it from later, but perhaps it helped me become aware of the word as I understand it today.

My angle then had more to do with language and communication, than with the more general significance of curiosity as the driving force behind progress.

Can you be curious about curiosity, or is that gilding the lily? Do you in that case end up in a never-ending circle? If you're curious about something, without having found the answer, you can, of course, assume an answer and renew your curiosity on that basis.

I've always been into technical challenges and have in all modesty found solutions to various of such challenges. As you can see, I prefer to call them challenges instead of problems, and these solutions have led to both patents and the manufacture of new products.

The expression "problems" is negative, whereas the word "challenges" trigger solutions.

This sidestepping is another matter altogether, but I'm convinced that everyone who has had anything to do with product development will agree, that to find satisfaction in this field you must be curious and look at "why?" from the above-mentioned angle.

Curiosity is the driving force behind progress.

I'm curious as to whether anyone has got anything sensible out of this, but I'm not really interested enough to ask. It could result in my having a set-back, which would reduce my curiosity and, as you may have understood, I would rather not lose it.

MY FOOD FOR THOUGHT ON CURIOSITY

CURIOSITY

Curiosity is the driving force behind progress.
2013

CURIOSITY ABOUT LIFE

You can well be Curious about Life and at the same time have a nature that is nailed to the earth.
2017

CURIOUS AND INDIFFERENT

Curiosity is the door opener for any development - while Indifference gives rise to stagnation.

IN MY HEAD

In my Head there's a diode with thread -
and behind my look so quick, there's many a click.
To adjust, open and shut - the free circulation must never be cut.

FANATICISM

May 2014

Even though it's probably clear to most of us what fanaticism means, I'll start, just in case, with a description from Wikipedia, which says that fanaticism is: "Extreme one-track mindedness. Enthusiastic claiming of personal convictions, often combined with wanting to persecute those who think or feel differently".

It almost makes me shudder when the word fanaticism is read or heard, or even just by thinking about it. Only in very special cases can I find something positive in connection with fanaticism, and then it has to do with personal fanaticism, for instance, when you are fanatically concerned about something special. In most cases, that kind of fanaticism is probably completely harmless.

Its limits are clear for most of us, but not for everyone, and that is probably what makes fanaticism so dangerous.

What I find somewhat strange is that one English description of fanaticism is in line with the above, in other words with the personal and harmless one. It goes like this: "Fanaticism is a belief or attitude involving uncritical eagerness or exaggerated enthusiasm as regards past-time activities or hobbies". Well, if that had been the only angle of fanaticism, lots of things would be different.

Many have tried throughout time to analyse the fanatic, he or she who stands for fanaticism. When that happens, it has mainly to do with that which most of us consider dangerous fanaticism.

The consensus seems to be that fanatics as such aren't

evil in the strict sense of the word: they, the fanatics, are just fanatically convinced that the opinions they represent are the only correct ones. There is never any talk of compromise, seen from a fanatic's point of view, so the idea of using diplomacy where the fanatic is concerned, can be shelved at once. The greatest danger lies in the fanatic's ability to influence the weak or misguided, examples of which we see every day.

Well, of course, I'm not competent to add anything at all as regards fanaticism, but, on the other hand, I am concerned about having to put an end to this evil, the dangerous one, that is, once and for all. We must be realistic though, to believe that we can get rid of the dangerous fanaticism, is to aim too high.

If you want to try to do that, you must apply other measures, at least if you have a long-term solution in mind. Just imagine finding a sensible answer to that challenge.

In many areas it is totally acceptable to refer to statistics.

Of course, you can't always trust the statistics, but that has nothing to do with those involved not being able to gather the right material, but with the fact that the material has been manipulated for the statistics to show the desired result.

Regardless, there must be a statistic showing the percentage of the population who are fanatical according to the definition. I don't doubt that at all, but I believe there is a reluctance to making it official. It could lead to social consequences.

Is the percentage of people who are fanatical according to the definition – the dangerous one if it can be isolated –, greater, or smaller than five percent; or is it more than ten percent?

Is the percentage of the population who are fanatical according to the definition described in the English interpretation, greater or smaller than five percent, or is it more than ten percent? Would our knowing the size of the percentage have any significance at all for the rest of us in our daily lives?

Personally, I believe there are far more fanatics amongst us than we believe. In fact, I'd go so far as putting myself down as a potential candidate, as regards to the English interpretation, the one I believe to be harmless.

How can I say that? Well, there are things in our everyday lives that I can be fanatically concerned about, without my wanting to tell what they are.

This is because it has nothing to do with a permanent condition, and because I know that this form of fanaticism is a completely harmless one, at least for others. Whether it might be dangerous for me is another matter.

What I'm trying to say, in other words, is that fanaticism as such isn't necessarily dangerous. It's only if it's used incorrectly, according to most of us, that it becomes dangerous.

The dangerous fanatic is usually someone who chooses his followers with great care. Trust is created and solid friendships are made. The followers are usually simple and easily influenced people, and thus fit easily into the role of performing the evil transmitted through the relationship. In this role the fanatic is mortally dangerous.

If we stay with this latter description, of the dangerous fanatic, I trust that an honest statistic would verify that only a fraction of one percent of the population belongs to this category, at least in our part of the world, which is a good thing, if my assumption is correct.

Even if there is little each one of us can do to expose these potential “bomb threats”, it is important that we make our beliefs and attitudes clear, so that we and those of like minds won’t be subjected to unexpected ambushes.

MY FOOD FOR THOUGHT ON FANATICISM

FANATICISM AND OPINIONS

There is certainly a great deal of agreement that Fanatics as such are not evil, in the true meaning of the word. Fanatics are just Fanatically convinced that the Opinions they have are the only correct ones.

May 2014

THE FANATIC'S ENFORCER

The dangerous Fanatic is a good listener who carefully choose his Enforcer. Trust is created and solid ties are made. Enforcers usually consists of simple and easy-to-influence people, who thus act perfectly in the role as practitioners of the evil transmitted through the relationship with the Fanatic.

May 2014

FANATICISM I

There is never any question of compromise from the Fanatic's point of view, so, the idea of using diplomacy to resolve a conflict involving the Fanatic can be shelved immediately.

2014

FANATICISM II

There is probably little that each of us can do to expose these possible "bomb threats", but it is important that we have our attitude clear, so that we and our like-minded people do not become the subject of unexpected ambushes.

2014

FEELING OF GUILT

April 2013

A feeling of guilt; it makes me shudder just thinking of it. Not that I believe I have reason to feel guilty, but there's no doubt that I'm one of those people who gives off an aura of guilt. This being the case even though I, at least in my own opinion, have no reason to do so.

Perhaps it has something to do with my adolescence.

I used to toe the line in my youth. There were seldom serious wrongdoings, but there was something about having to try things out. It's important to find out where to draw the line, as parents don't always offer appropriate guidelines.

If you are born with imagination and empathy, consequences are bound to follow.

My stepfather had a clear idea of where the line had to be drawn, everything he saw as a serious wrongdoing was measured in a certain number of strokes from the dog whip: it was as simple as that.

In many situations this is probably a good method of settling things, but according to today's standards apparently far from the right one. We mustn't forget that this was more than sixty years ago, and a lot was different in those days.

Enough said, I believe that I found the punishment just at the time. If I had crossed the line, that was the price I had to pay. Otherwise, the only alternative I could see to avoid the punishment was to run away from home. I don't believe that would have solved anything. I also don't believe my mother was quite in tune with the punishments but having a domineering husband, she chose to keep peace on the home front. At least I never registered any arguments between them on this subject. The threat of being sent to the correctional institution on Bastøy in the Oslo fjord also remained in the background but was from my side probably never seen as a real possibility. In my opinion, that would be like shooting sparrows with a cannon. Nor did it ever happen.

We probably all experience a feeling of guilt in some form or other. You only have to look around among your family and friends. Whether the feeling of guilt is justified, only the person involved can say.

When I mentioned earlier on that those feelings of guilt may have to do with my adolescence, I was perhaps quite wrong. My younger half-sister, who never did anything wrong when she was little, has undoubtedly all her adult life had problems with her feelings of guilt. Could it have something to do with one's nature and not with one's nurture?

In my case, the conscious feeling of guilt first occurred at school. There's no reason to hide that I was a so-called trouble- maker in class, but it was, as far as I remember, never suggested that whatever I did had a nasty intent.

It's strange to see, but my youngest grandchild, who is fifteen this year, has apparently had the same sort of struggle at school for the last few years. I have been given to understand that he is undoubtedly also a mischief-maker in class.

I have no difficulty facing reality today, and I see that many of the reprimands were justified.

But what about the other side of the coin? Often because of the above, you automatically got accused of things you hadn't done or taken part in? That was sometimes hard to swallow. It was thus registered as deeply unfair and difficult to understand.

So, I ask myself the question: is there a clear link between in- justice and feelings of guilt? I can't quite come to grips with it, but I have a feeling I'm on to something essential here.

This probably won't stop me using injustice as a separate theme for a reflection. It is, after all, a huge subject to write about when you think about all the injustice there is in the world.

Regardless, my feeling of guilt has fortunately decreased over the years.

At one time, I could never go through passport control with- out being called aside for a closer check.

The customs officers had a special eye for me, almost as if I were some sort of regular problem to them. I can't remember ever having been caught carrying anything I shouldn't have, or my "quota" having been exceeded. I don't want anyone to consider me sanctimonious in this context, but just because I believe my bad conscience could be sensed from afar, it was a contributing factor to my never carrying anything more than that which was within the allowable limits. This applies to the present as well as the past.

I mentioned the possible link between injustice and feelings of guilt, but now conscience comes into play.

I've already written a reflection about conscience. In it there is something about suppressing your feelings of a bad conscience and the warm glow you get from a good one. Conscience probably belongs in this reflection too, because I don't suppose there's anything called good or bad feelings of guilt, is there?

After this, the question will have to be changed to: is there a link between injustice, conscience and feelings of guilt?

It is time to get off this track before I start spinning out of control, as so far it has become complicated enough.

As some of you will have noticed, apart from my half-sister, it has so far only been about my own relationship to feelings of guilt. The reason for this must be that it is virtually impossible to describe other people's feeling of guilt, as that's a very private matter.

MY FOOD FOR THOUGHT ON FEELINGS OF GUILT

FEELINGS OF GUILT I

We all have Feelings of Guilt in one form or another. If this feeling is justified or not, only the person with the Guilt can comment on.

May 2019

FEELING OF GUILT II

No one can describe the Feeling of Guilt of others.

May 2019

GUILT AND INNOCENCE

The feeling of Guilt is hard to bear - while the weight of Innocence is light as a feather.

FAULT

What would the world look like if we had no one to blame?

Oct. 2019

IGNORANCE

Oct. 2013

Why on earth am I dwelling on this word. Fortunately, it isn't used all that much, but when it is, it's usually in a serious context. If it is so that, in our daily life, we connect ignorance with stupidity, as I believe we tend to do, then that's wrong, in which case it might be worthwhile immersing ourselves a bit in ignorance.

I don't in any way wish to compete with Wikipedia or others who, in page after page, present all sorts of interpretations of the word. Perhaps I see something contradictory in the interpretations I'm dwelling on.

If ignorance has something to do with ignore, which sounds reasonable, it might seem a bit affected to say that to ignore means something like: "to refuse to take into account", whereas ignorance is described among other things as: "to pretend not to be aware of or know anything about this or that, or to be indifferent to".

If you look at the word ignorant, which must also have something to do with ignorance, then it is described, among other things, as: "to lack information about or knowledge of this and that". And in this context also: "to lack education or to be unsophisticated".

The word ignorant is further described as: "a person who is in a state of not being in the know; often used as an insult to describe those who ignore or discount important information or facts on purpose". I see this as being the same as: "to express yourself against better judgement".

It already becomes difficult for the average person to

keep up, and these are only a few simple approaches.

I would probably not have started grappling with ignorance if I hadn't had a few experiences of my own related to the word. These I won't refer to, neither with names or situations, but more with attitudes, which I'm sure several people can identify with, either by doing a self-analysis or by examining their own experiences.

The ostrich is reputed to put its head in the sand when it senses danger. It then is supposed to believe itself to be invisible and thus can't be noticed. The ostrich is claimed to believe it is less visible and therefore feels safer, so what then has the ostrich got to do with my experiences of ignorance?

Well, even well-educated people, who are in no way stupid, can in certain situations act with ignorance.

Complete information can be available in all aspects of a case. It is also known with reasonable certainty that the people concerned do have all the information.

External indoctrination probably also plays an important role when it comes to behaviour patterns.

It happens again and again, however, that behaviour pattern shows that actual, available information is completely set aside, in other words, ignored, a fact which invariably displays ignorance on the part of those concerned. Or does it?

Is this then deliberate, or does it just happen? Is it a form of possible protection, like the ostrich act, or is it a fully conscious act? Again, we must make clear that: "Ignorance differs from stupidity, though both can lead to unwise actions".

As far as my own experiences goes, I choose to believe that some actions weren't fully conscious. Because when I choose to believe that the actions were deliberate, the whole thing takes on a more serious aspect, which might lead to much more serious consequences.

Good thing I'm tolerant.

Their actions are fully conscious. They know that they are talking against their better judgement, as that is what is necessary at times; it is this which, in my opinion, is unfortunate. Can it be described as a form of dishonesty?

If I stick to the earlier description of the word ignorant: "a person who is in a state of not being in the know; often used as an insult to describe those who ignore or discount important information or facts", then it's the one I adhere to when it comes to my own experiences.

Knowing full well that I may have misunderstood some details in my interpretation of ignorance, I'm right, at least according to my own assumptions. If you're curious as to what I mean by that, you can look at one of my earlier reflections: "What is right and what is wrong?".

I must admit, however, that even though I wasn't conscious of it, I may, in a pinch, have used this form of ignorance myself.

It wouldn't surprise me if to "express yourself against your better judgement" is considerably more widespread than I've assumed.

MY FOOD FOR THOUGHT ON IGNORANCE

IGNORANCE I

A description of the word is: "To pretend that you don't know about this or that, or to be indifferent." Otherwise, intelligent people, in special contexts, can act with ignorance. Fully accessible information is present when it comes to all sides of a case, and it is known with reasonable certainty that those concerned are in possession of this information. Still, they speak out "against their better judgment".

October 2013

IGNORANCE II

If Ignorance has something to do with ignoring, it might seem a bit far-fetched that ignoring supposedly also means: "To refuse to pay attention to".

October 2013

THE OSTRICH GAME

The ostrich is known to bury its head in the sand when it is in danger. It thereby believes that it is invisible and is not noticed. The fact is that it is, of course, just as visible, while the self-deception makes it safe. If people who speak out against their better judgment are aware of what they are doing, the result can have serious consequences.

October 2013

IGNORANCE AND STUPIDITY

Ignorance differs from Stupidity, although both can lead to unwise actions.

October 2013

LIFE

2016

Life - who can describe life?

Life has different values in various cultures, and in some it seems like it has no value at all.

Fortunately, we know very little about life, apart from that it starts and at an unpredictable time ends.

In addition, another thing we know about it is that all of us are living it in one or another way, as long as we live. Most probably we live it as individually different as there are people on this earth, or, put in another way, as there are different fingerprints.

Some have big ambitions in life while others don't seem conscious of that property at all.

We are all different, arriving from different environments and belonging to different religions.

We live under different climates, belong to different forms of societies, and perform different tasks in the society we belong to.

Some claim that they are eligible to a larger portion of social benefits than others, and claim they deserve it, while others deal with the situation as it is and are happy that way.

Some need showing strength to keep their self-esteem, while others fully obey rules and regulations drawn up for what's right and wrong.

Others again, act as if they were the ones making the rules and regulations.

We all want to live, or at least most of us.

But when life is on its way to come to an end for whatever reason, and you are still conscious and clear, do you miss something? Specially if it happens at a young age.

You may at that stage not yet have got the big overview.

Do you ever in life get the big overview, and what might that consist of?

Even if you believe that you have found the answer to the big overview, will there still be something you miss, something you feel has not been done?

This theme is undoubtedly so personal, and its meanings so many, that it leads nowhere to go further.

Apart from that, you should not dwell too much on it either; time comes soon enough when too many of these thoughts come to mind.

When that happens it's presumably good, at least for some, to think about the life you have led, and how you have made use of it. Because that is life itself.

Is it likely that you ever get the big overview, and will you ever know what you missed?

"What is life, a breath in the sea, which descends……" by Adam Oehlenschlæger, is one most of us have heard about.

Søren Kirkegaard has a wonderful description of life:

"The day you came to the world, you cried while your close ones were happy. Live life so that the day you die, your close ones will cry while you're happy".

Imagine how simple things would be if we stopped worrying.

Samuel Johnson is in his full right stating:

"It's useless to worry about life; you won't get out of it alive anyhow"

I don't know who was the first one with this, but for me it has, for a long time, been a good rule of life that:

"Problems do not exist, only challenges".

"Live life as if you are going to die tomorrow" is a saying.

To me this sounds rather dramatic.

Should you fully follow this rule, you could be personally guilty in your short stay on mother earth.

If it is correct that most of us agree that life is an art of balance, something at least I advocate for, then maybe my own formulation in various ways illustrates this.

"Life is like a continuous surf. You must keep your balance until you reach land. Only then is it over".

After having written the above, it strikes me that so far, I have only mentioned life in conjunction with us people - extremely egocentric.

Our lives would of course not have existed if we were the only living creatures on earth.

After all, we are only one form of life among millions.

I'm not thinking about a life comparable with ours, but all forms of life needed to keep us humans going.

This is probably too much to comprehend.

We must only accept that, in one or another form, we are created, that we are a tiny little part of a whole, and that all life is dependent on one another.

The following "slogans" used these days in some TV channels, are a reminder in this context.

"If nature is not kept healthy, humans won't survive"; and the other from the nature: "If you don't take care of me, I can't take care of you".

Unfortunately, we humans are putting too much of a load on nature. Admittedly, at times we pull ourselves together and try to clean up misery, but only when we realise that we have let it go too far. That however is not good enough.

Maybe it's time we extend our thoughts about life from being egocentric "us selves first", to seriously consider how we – having the ability to act, after all – can do something to keep a continuous balance in nature.

In this context, it must be added that a big group of us devote ourselves to improving our relationship to nature, which is good if it doesn't become fanatic.

We must never forget that if war breaks out between nature and ourselves, we will, no doubt, be the losers. There are plenty of challenges.

In my 78th year (2016) I reached the view that our cycle as individuals on this earth is magnificently adapted to our development.

Through our life we are constantly developing.

If we live long enough, we will see next generations starting where we left off, knowing that they will go through the same development as we did.

I don't believe those advocating that we can learn from experience gained by others. In life we must all gain experience ourselves, at times in a heavy way, not from others.

MY FOOD FOR THOUGHT ON LIFE

LIFE I

The best thing about Life is that it's yours. The most difficult can be to acknowledge it, take the initiative and do something about it.

To my daughter Anne-Marie on her 20th birthday

LIFE II

The only thing we know about Life is that it's lived by all of us, in one form or other, as long as we Live.

2016

LIFE III

If you mean Life is different than you think, you are wrong.

Aug. 2019

LIFE UNTIL NOW

Until now I've lived Life - and experienced Life.

1995

OPINIONS

April 2014

If you haven't got an opinion about anything at all, you are, in my opinion, seemingly lost. Most of us, however, have opinions about most things, but having opinions isn't worth much if you don't know how to express them.

To have opinions and to be able to express them if you so wish is, at least in those democracies I'm familiar with, a privilege worth fighting for.

It is a human right which should never be taken for granted. We have all seen tragic examples of suppressed freedom of expression.

No debate on my part about freedom of expression; it ought to be taken for granted in an enlightened world, but the way I see it, that's not unfortunately the case everywhere.

Even though there is freedom of expression, it isn't necessarily so that when you have an opinion about something, you must express it, put things bluntly or fight on the barricades it.

Furthermore, to keep certain opinions to oneself is a piece of advice I would like to give to all those who tend to spill over with them.

I don't believe that so-called normal people exist who don't have opinions about anything at all; everyone probably has opinions, it's part of the pulse of life.

On the other hand, those who have so-called convictions are perhaps few and far between. Anyway, as I've said, you don't need to fight for all your opinions, but when you have so-called hobby horses, understood to mean things you feel strongly about, then it's good to have convictions. It means that you stand by your opinions and fight for them.

Here you must, as in so many other contexts, be aware of the challenges connected to what many of us see as fanatical opinions and attitudes; but that's a totally different matter.

Fanaticism we'll put to one side in this case. It is scary enough as we've seen many examples of. Fanaticism is unfortunately everywhere, in all social, political, and religious fractions, and exists in almost all contexts. There is no doubt that we, for ever or at least for as long as human beings rule our world, will become acquainted with this unpleasant evil, fanaticism.

In early adolescence it is normally so that many of us are concerned with choosing what is right, according to the opinion of others, for fear of being looked upon as outsiders. Human beings are, as far as I know, defined as "pack animals", in this case to be understood as having identical beliefs: it makes us feel secure.

As you gradually start to feel comfortable with your life and more secure in yourself, you will form your own opinions about certain things, which will differ from those of others.

This I believe is related to the interests you have or acquire, but it is probably also a result of social and cultural influences. In many ways this is all well and good, as it is the fact that we aren't all the same, which adds spice to our respective lives.

We have something to compare with when, or better put if we can see our own opinions in relation to existing general norms. Many great personalities throughout time have had firm opinions about almost everything, which I believe is both reasonable and correct. Even though their opinions didn't always turn out to be the right ones, that's how it must be.

In order not to make the case too close to our time, we can use an example which goes back almost two thousand years in time. The then Roman Senator, Cato the Elder, is said to have ended all his speeches in the Senate with the subsequently famous sentence, here translated into English: "Furthermore I believe Carthage must be destroyed".

The reason for this was allegedly that he believed the city's wealth to be a threat to Rome.

Well, we can only hope that Cato the Younger, that is if he existed, learnt from this.

I have fought without success against firm collective opinions, virtually bordering on the fanatic. Whatever touch of diplomatic attitude I might have, immediately came up short, but it became a very special experience.

The time is the late eighties, and the place is Cabrera, the urbanization in the south of Spain where I had just begun my long-term plan to establish myself, when my retirement age was invariably reached – if I managed to live that long, that was.

I had already made good contact with the establisher and developer of the place, a very charismatic English architect, a good fifteen years older than myself. His name was Peter Grosscurth.

Unrealistic laws, or perhaps the lack of the same in Spain, were, as far as I could understand, both unclear and flexible at the time. A great deal of improvising was required to get the books to balance in this context, and it didn't help that additions and changes took place continuously, with or without retroactive effect.

Enough said, the above-mentioned Peter had on-going challenges with the inhabitants who had already established themselves in the urbanization, as to which of the various common expenses they had to bear, as well as several practical details to do with the development itself. Practically speaking, this meant that a lot of them didn't pay anything at all.

As extenuating circumstances for those implicated, it must be mentioned that language and communication problems, as well as an understanding of the legislation, played a part.

One day, as Peter and I sat talking about the problem, which to me seemed totally crazy, I proposed that I make an objective attempt at mediating the conflict. After some decades as leader of a family business with more than 150 employees, I believed myself to possess a certain amount of experience in human relationships. The day came when I had gathered thirty or forty of the protesting clan for an information meeting. Food and drink had been organized and the atmosphere was good from the start. Peter was obviously not there, so it was just me and all the rest.

I had prepared myself well, I thought, and had committed everything to paper in order that nothing be left to chance.

Everyone listened without any form of interruption, and I felt that I had good control of the situation.

I believe my speech lasted about ten minutes whereupon I opened for a discussion about the arguments.

A few questions, for the sake of understanding, were raised here and there and answered, before I asked everyone to respect the laws referring to everyone having to share the communal expenses, to secure the future value of their respective investments.

After a short time where we continued the discussion in groups, one of them came over to see me and said something like: "George, I speak on behalf of all of us. We largely agree with your argumentation and that you have put your case well, but you can tell Peter from all of us that we won't pay anything at all, before we are threatened by law to do so."

Neither before nor after have I heard such a collective opinion on something from so many different types of people.

What I didn't know at the time, however, but which later became clear to me, was that these people, who were mainly English, had previously been stationed in different countries around the world and had now settled here as pensioners. As the prices in Spain had already at this time made a great leap upwards, their economic situation had reached its breaking point.

In other words, it probably wasn't so much a lack of will as of possibility, and then, of course, it's important to maintain one's prestige.

It eventually ended up with many of the properties changing owners, and I don't really know what became of the hard core, but I hope at least that those who are still living after some twenty-five years, are doing well.

The regulations came into place eventually, the urbanization was fully legalized and these days it's neither misunderstood laws nor the government's responsibility that you are still doing battle – but so it is.

In the final analysis, people's divergent opinions, based on their different views on most things, is the reason for the on-going challenges in this little oasis. Fractions are formed and contrary views are put to the test.

For those of you who think this is an exception, take a closer look with this in mind, and see if it isn't also your opinion that this is reflected everywhere.

MY FOOD FOR THOUGHT ON OPINIONS

OPINION

You should decide early if you want to be remembered with a good reputation or put all your energy into living.

March 2019

OPINIONS I

My Opinion is that it can be a good rule of thumb to keep your Opinions to yourself and not be tempted to express them unless you are sure they will not cause offence.

July 2020

OPINIONS II

It's good to have Opinions on most things - but only if you don't claim they are the best.

Sept. 2019

OPINIONS III

Having opinions and being able to express them if you so wish is, at least in the democracies I know of, a privilege worth fighting for. It is a human right that must never be taken for granted.

2014

THE SMILE
May 1994

The smile gives you a feeling of warmth. It's always a relief when the smile appears, whether it's you yourself who are smiling or someone else.

Some people seem to be smiling permanently. It's not that kind of smile I'm thinking of, however; that kind seems to belong to an entire race of people, like in the Orient for instance.

No, I'm thinking of the smile we see daily on people we socialize with. That smile which you yourself, perhaps to a far greater extent than you do, should bring out.

The smile is warming, gives you a feeling of security. It's difficult to make contact with people who don't smile.

They don't necessarily suppress their smile on purpose, they probably are like that, don't understand the importance of the smile, in which case I feel sorry for them.

"Smile courses". Once again, we're talking about the smile which isn't so natural.

Millions and millions are spent by companies and organizations to promote themselves in a more positive way.

This is probably positive and perhaps even motivating for the employees. That's also not the kind of smile I'm thinking of, however.

The smile is something so personal, that if you have the slightest feeling it might not be real, it has a negative impact; you must be certain that the smile is real.

Be it from the slightly condescending smile we're all familiar with, to the one which stretches from ear to ear - the range is incredibly wide.

I've never thought about what the smile would be like without the eyes, but this reflection is not really about the eyes, it's about the smile.

Are we so used to the interaction between the eyes and the smile that it would be difficult to read expressions without that interaction, that is, with the smile alone?

I'll have to keep thinking about that.

Perhaps it's unfair to focus on the smile just on its own? Can the smile stand alone, be enough by itself?

Smile and the world smiles back at you, it is said.

There must be a lot of people who don't want the world smiling back at them.

MY FOOD FOR THOUGHT ON THE SMILE

THE SMILE

A Smile is like sand on ice, it helps you walk more safely.

THE SMILE AND INSECURITY

The Smile is personal. If you feel Insecurity about its authenticity, it's negative. You must be sure that the Smile is genuine.

THE SMILE II

"Smile and the world smiles back at you at you", is a saying. There must be quite a few who do not want the world to smile on them.

May 1994

THE SMILE III

The smile warms, in a way gives a feeling of security. It's hard to connect with people who don't smile. It is not at all certain that they suppress the smile on purpose, they may just be like that, they don't understand the meaning of the smile. In that case, I pity them.

May 1994

THE SOUL

April 1994

It's not easy to write about the soul - at least not when you have lost it. Not the soul itself, of course, but what I meant to write about it.

My dictation about the soul has been lost - it's just gone - it's good that it wasn't the soul itself that got lost.

Something as important as souls shouldn't be able to become lost - disappear - at least, not easily.

A dictation doesn't get lost either unless you make a mistake. In my eagerness to dictate some reflections about something so trivial as a "water-pipe" - yes, just a normal "water-pipe" - I happened to dictate on top of the soul - and it disappeared.

I had just taken a bath which made me think of the "water-pipe".

I grab my Pocket Memo and start - discovering too late that the soul had been rewound and that my reflections about the "water-pipe", had taken the place of the soul.

Could hardly have been worse - not for the soul - but for me. My poor brain barely remembers bits of what I had dictated - pity.

It was, in fact, quite good - at least according to the woman I played it back to. Easy to say now that the proof is gone.

The soul lives on. Some of the best things I meant to write about the soul, I'll remember as I go along - putting pen to paper. It made me more than a little nervous when I discovered that I'd dictated on top of the soul.

This is consequently written without a prior dictation.

It's like being in an accident - just something I've heard - but it's supposed to be essential to put yourself as quickly as possible in a similar situation - or, it is said, you never will again.

It would be a pity if I stopped dictating for fear of losing what I dictate - not for the soul - it will go on living.

At least the one I'm talking about.

I'll continue to dictate.

It is said at home, for example, that my soul never returns from my travels when I do - it always gets there a day later.

It's not something I notice myself - I don't have a feeling of loss - I'm convinced that my soul is securely anchored in my body.

The question is what happens to the soul when it's time for the body to say good-bye.

Does the soul live on in art, literature, and music? Hardly - our Creator was probably a democrat - normal souls should also be given a chance.

It is said that houses have souls. This as an example of our apparent acceptance that also things have souls. Quite possibly – I don't believe it, and don't for a second doubt that, if that were the case, it would have to be a totally different type of soul - not the real soul – the one with a capital S.

Reflections on that soul, the one with a capital S, was what the dictation was all about. It wasn't especially mysterious - only expressed that it would be strange if there wasn't something more, something more than the life we "miserable" people lead here on earth.

I have several experiences behind me, which leave no doubt about the "great beyond".

Something else altogether is that I've never quite understood those who are always looking for their soul - searching for it, as if it were lost. They themselves must have convinced themselves that it's lost, or they wouldn't be searching for it.

Can the soul be lost - not in the form of a dictation or a piece of writing - and in that case, can it be found again?

What for instance does the soul do when we are sleeping? Does it also rest, or is that just what it doesn't do? Is it watching over us, making sure our body rests?

Even though the human body is a wonder all on its own, it must rest regardless how highly born - even Churchill had to rest, though he apparently didn't need much sleep.

What about his soul? Was it special? It is said that his body was filled with more than a bottle of whisky a day. Was his soul damaged by it?

No doubt the pleasure his body took in it wasn't undivided.

It is said that he was best suited to be a leader at wartime, under pressure: was his soul especially suited to the task?

I see from this that there are several things I must do some more thinking about.

Something isn't quite right. Expressions like a great

soul, a brave soul, an anxious soul, a rotten soul, a divided soul – how does it all fit together?

I'm sure I'll remember some of the things I dictated about the soul – that which was lost – when my subconscious is working. It was good after all.

If the soul separates from the body when we pass on, the soul must go somewhere: the body disappears - that's concrete - but the soul?

Regardless, there must be some greater meaning to it all. I don't need the testimony of a theologian to understand that the soul with a capital S exists.

MY FOOD FOR THOUGHT ON THE SOUL

THE SOUL

I do not need the theologians' testimony to understand that we have a "Soul" with a capital S.

THE SOUL II

Is it the case that the Soul lives on in art, literature, and music?
Hardly - Our Creator was a democrat.
Ordinary Souls should also have a chance.
April 1994

THE SOUL III

I have never understood those who are constantly looking for their Soul, looking for it, as if it were lost. They themselves must be convinced that it is lost, otherwise they wouldn't be looking for it, would they?
April 1994

THE SOUL IV

If Soul and body split when we pass away, the Soul must go somewhere. The body does disappear - that is concrete - but what about the Soul?
1994

THOUGHTS

October 1995

Are they just there or do we do something to make them appear?

My experience is that it's difficult to keep them in order, and that has probably something to do with concentration.

My thoughts race past in a constant flickering motion. When I put it like that, it's because I feel that there is a marked interaction between my thoughts and the visual image on my retina. I've never asked anyone else if they feel the same way.

It's a wonder that your thoughts don't boil over at times, but where would they go if they did?

You do, however, feel at times as though your thoughts are like steam in a pressure cooker, don't you? Especially when they are thoughts you have brooded over for a long time. They want out in one form or other and out they normally get.

Can, for instance, a burst of anger be the actual safety valve for a collection of aggressive thoughts?

If you are totally relaxed and just let your thoughts flow, which thoughts get priority, and which ingenious system does the prioritizing?

Is this where the subconscious comes into it? Is it just another storehouse for thoughts?

Is it so that if you don't consciously suppress certain thoughts, you will be left with an even distribution of the different types?

It is undoubtedly a lot more pleasant to conjure up

good thoughts, than to struggle with a predominance of bad ones. The latter can easily become a great strain if it happens over time.

The question is if it can be so easily controlled.

Here I believe it's important that you in yourself are reasonably balanced and that you have a platform to stand on, which isn't too slippery, and which gives your feet a good grip.

Thoughts are tax-free, it is said. It's important to take note of that.

It's a privilege we all have as human beings, that we can keep our thoughts to ourselves.

No one will ever get to know what you are thinking about if you want to keep it to yourself.

To share your thoughts with others can be good.

How often do we say: "Think of the time". Here you refer to thoughts about something or other, which you assume the person you are addressing has shared or heard about.

When you experience someone reading your thoughts, or when you feel that you yourself can read someone else's thoughts, it's probably more random or a result of being closely connected to the person and, thus, able to read his or her body language.

In connection with thoughts, I come to think about how good I feel right now.

Lying here relaxing after a hot bath and giving my thoughts free rein.

MY FOOD FOR THOUGHT ON THOUGHTS

THOUGHTS I

It is more pleasant to conjure up good Thoughts than to struggle with bad ones. The latter can become a strain if it becomes the norm.

1995

THOUGHTS II

When you struggle with Thoughts, they are normally both good and bad. Let your Thoughts flow freely when that happens; blockages can cause flooding.

May 2019

THOUGHTS III

It's said that "Thoughts are tax-free". Luckily so, otherwise I would be a poor man.

April 2019

THOUGHTS AND STEAM

Thoughts can be like Steam in a pressure cooker. They shall come out in some form or other.

Oct. 1995

UNDERSTANDING II

2017

The wish of understanding and will to understand is fundamental. If you wish not to understand or reject the thought of understanding, no understanding is achieved, and so you can't expect to be understood either. You must have the wish and will to understand, to achieve understanding. In other words, understanding requires both wish and will.

Do you come further with understanding? After my opinion undoubtedly yes.

All decisions, if they should have any validity, must be based on understanding, and the wish and will to understand the content of the matter and the parties involved.

In many cases, it is much easier to keep the understanding in the background, not to use will, force and time to understand. Then, however the probability is great for the decisions to be of poor quality.

Imagine that it is so simple.

Pundits are normally easy to understand. They often express simple, understandable postulates about this and that, but thanks to their personality they are normally categorised as unsympathetic.

Those, who on the other side acts consciously and keep the more modest style will normally be both respected and appreciated.

"Do you understand"? An expression often used when you expect a confirmation that the message is understood.

In my opinion, it can be too much on the commanding side. You take it for granted that the message is understood.

A “yes” is expected as a confirmation.

For many it becomes difficult to say no, even if that is what they mean. For the one party this is of course correct, but what about the quality of the understanding.

Why not try with a little more weakened question? “I hope you have understood”. This gives full admission to grasp eventual insecurity and may result in the following answer: “Yes, but I have a few questions”. The dialogue is on, understanding substantiated, the communication is balanced, and basis laid for a compromised result.

Nit-picking many will say, especially in these times of SMS and e-mail where the most advanced communicators use a minimum of words with associated probability of misunderstandings. These days it has even gone so as that some TV channels squeeze information or messages into one line. To achieve this all kind of abbreviations are used, making it meaningless for us ordinary people. What happened to understanding? Well, the ones that understand it.

Most probably, only those of us of a “vintage age” are the ones who sigh. Every now and then, in debates, you will recognise someone assessing the following entry as an answer to a statement.

“I have a great deal of understanding for what you are saying, but…”

Well, I suppose it won’t last long before this expression also disappears. It’s much easier to say it directly: “I disagree with what you are saying”.

I hope for some understanding of my view on the importance of understanding.

MY FOOD FOR THOUGHT ON UNDERSTANDING II

UNDERSTANDING IV

You can only do something with what you understand, but don't forget that what you understand is seen from your point of view.

April 2021

UNDERSTANDING V

Understanding is one of the most important words we have. What do you do with it?

June 2021

UNDERSTANDING VI

It is when you don't understand that you don't understand that the real challenges start.

July 2021

UNDERSTANDING VII

The fact that you think others do not understand does not mean that you are right in your own conviction that you are right.

September 2020

RIGHT AND WRONG

August 1990

Or should the question rather be: who is right and who is wrong? Yes, because that's really what most disputes are about. I simply claim that all of us are right based on our assumptions.

Is it thus as simple as saying that if everyone's assumptions were the same, you would no longer have any dispute about who is right or who is wrong? In other words, everyone would agree - thus no dispute.

Sounds simple, but so very far from reality.

Assumptions can be about possessing information. Then it naturally must be about interpreting the same information as well.

In this context it's natural to involve personal abilities and skills, as well as cultural and political backgrounds.

It's already clear to everyone that we're banging our heads against a brick wall - we just must admit that "all of us are right based on our assumptions".

Some – perhaps most of us –, think that we see something more clearly than others and thus believe I know what's right and the others are wrong.

That is, of course, nice to be able to think about when going into the depth of things – or isn't it?

I believe most of us agree on this.

And now that we've reached the stage of awareness, what do we do?

Do we leave things as they are in our self-aggrandizement? That is, of course, the easiest, after all, we know deep down that we are right, don't we? And what it means is that the others are wrong, or does it?

If we are distant from the problems, we sneer a bit and add have you ever heard such nonsense; or, they can't possibly have a clue about what they're doing.

Such thoughts become easier the further away from the problems you are.

If the problems are of a more familiar character, it hurts in a different way and we are more careful of making our, at times, casual remarks.

Should we now ask ourselves the question: can I do something to influence, can I do something to soften the extremes?

A good expression is that "the truth normally lies somewhere in the middle".

What sort of skills are necessary to find the truth?

No, now he's getting completely off course. The truth doesn't exist, at least not if it diverges from my view.

Oops - here it comes again.

Can the word "objectivity" be used?

Let's chew on it a bit - objectivity - objectivity.

Doesn't it mean: seen with unbiased eyes; without taking sides; impartial; seen from the outside; bridging the gap?

Not bad, is it?

Imagine being able to withdraw, stand apart, and from that position calmly look at the problem.

Imagine being able to look at both sides; being self-critical as regards the information and thus the assumptions you hold about the case.

Imagine being big enough to let the one who seems to "swim the hardest" get the benefit of the doubt, before stating your conclusions.

Yes, imagine!

Isn't this what is, in other words, called mediation?

Is that why they're called diplomats, those strange people we normally only see in a black Mercedes with blue plates?

Are they called diplomats because they're trying to bridge the gap between countries, cultures, and religions?

Of course, that's why; we know it.

Yes, but then most of us know that they mainly talk incomprehensible gibberish, don't we?

Or is it like that?

No, let's just try to act a bit more objectively in our day-to-day lives, be a bit more diplomatic perhaps, just in a few situations each week.

Each one of us needn't stretch further before seeing that the world would be a far better place to live in.

P.S. Notice that in this Reflection, which I wrote in 1990, i.e. almost 35 years ago, I have mentioned the word "problem" four times. I have long since replaced the word "problem" with "challenge", which is what the eight Food for Thought on the next pages are about.

MY FOOD FOR THOUGHT ON RIGHT AND WRONG

PROBLEM - CHALLENGE

A Problem can be complicated to solve. See the Problem as a challenge, and the solution becomes easier.

Sept. 2019

CHALLENGE IV

It's not just you who face Challenges, everyone does. It's the way you deal with them that's different.

Oct. 2019

PROBLEMS - CHALLENGES II

Everyone can recognize Problems when they see them. The art is to turn Problems into Challenges and to solve them.

PROBLEMS - CHALLENGES III

If you replace Problems with Challenges, it sounds much more positive. When faced with Challenges, the imagination is triggered, while the encounter with Problems may seem uninspiring.

March 2019

ABOUT BEING RIGHT

Why not swallow your pride, if that's how it feels when you admit that others are Right, and simply learn from it?
Why is it so important for most of us to be Right?
It's as if we constantly must convince ourselves that it is beneficial to be Right while it is a defeat to be wrong.

RIGHT AND WRONG I

My simple claim is that everyone is right based on their assumptions. Is it as simple as saying that if only everyone had the same assumptions, then we would no longer have the dispute about who is right and who is wrong?

August 1990

RIGHT AND WRONG II

Being right based on one's assumptions is about possessing information, and then of course it must also be about interpreting the same information.

August 1990

RIGHT AND WRONG III

I know what is right and wrong and it is the others who are wrong, many claim, and they feel good about that attitude. For them it is of course the easiest. They believe deep down that they are right, and that naturally means that the others are wrong. What they have forgotten, however, are the assumptions, namely that they are only right from their point of view.

August 199

YOU ARE ALONE

12 June 2015

This is not a statement about you being alone in the sense of not having family or friends close to you and loving you. A reasonably long experience has given me reasons to feel that I have both family and friends who appreciate me, so in the context of solitude I don't feel alone. The meaning of feeling alone I have in mind, is related to a challenge I am convinced quite a few of us have been facing.

At a certain time, in different contexts, you reach a point, or rather a peak, from which you normally can just look down to find an answer.

Why you only look down is logical because it's only down there you can see the tangible realities, as it's normally there you gained your experiences. If you look up there is just nothing.

In daytime, the impression you get can be grey and sad, but also bright and clear when the sun shines from a bright heaven.

The expression: "Over the clouds, the sun always shines", is a good reminder to lift the spirit a little.

If it's night and overcast, it's black; but if the night's cloudless you see endless amounts of stars, and often the moon as the largest light source.

For many, the answer to versatile challenges in life lies up there, whatever faith.

Many govern their life related to the contact they feel they have up there, independent of their religion.

For those it matters, it becomes okay and easy I should

think, even if the faith can be put to great tests.

Personally, I have had my fair part of challenges throughout life, and have as one of my slogans:

"It's mainly through challenges and how you tackle them, that you learn to advance. What relation each of us have to prayer must be kept as a private matter".

As my daughter and son-in-law took over the responsibility of the company, naturally enough it became their being confronted with unforeseen challenges

My son-in-law has a strong robust attitude to most and tackles his position impeccably.

I seldom give advice unless questioned, but there was one thing I tried to convey to him based on my own experience, right from the beginning. Whatever good employees you have, more often than you think, there will be situations where you are alone; it is up to you to take the final decision and there is no one you can ask but yourself.

As a result of that it's also you having to take the consequences of your decisions.

Situations will occur where, for good reason, only you have all information as it can't be shared with anyone.

That's what comes with being a responsible leader.

My son-in-law has, on several occasions, faced challenges where I reminded him about this; but so far, I have a certain impression of that not being necessary. I think he is aware of the matter and has a good understanding about the situation.

Many reading this might not totally understand or agree

that it is like this. Rightly, from their point of view they feel being valuable supporters, as by all means they are.

The same goes for board members. In the same way, they feel they have the job, amongst other because they give good advice. They also, from their point of view, do believe they are good advisers, and of course they are.

But – and that is an important but –, as I believe only can be understood by the ones with the ultimate responsibility: “Situations will occur where you stand totally alone”.

MY FOOD FOR THOUGHT ON YOU ARE ALONE

As you understand from the above Reflection, it is not about being alone physically, but being alone in making decisions or drawing conclusions that can have unforeseen consequences. The four Food for Thought that follows are based on that.

YOU ARE ALONE I

It is mostly only through challenges, and tackling them, that you learn to move on.

July 2023

YOU ARE ALONE II

Even if you have a close family and good friends, situations will arise more often than you think where you are alone with your decisions. It is you who must take them and there is only yourself to ask.

2015

YOU ARE ALONE III

Situations where you are alone can arise in cases where only you have all the information, which for good reasons cannot be shared with others.

2015

YOU ARE ALONE IV

There will always be situations where you are alone.

2015

TIME

April 1994

I'll do that when I retire, many people say; I'll have more time when I become a pensioner.

Nonsense. Do it now, I say.

That, of course, is impossible. It's only when you become a pensioner that you can do what you want to do now.

The decision seldom or never has to do with economy - always with time.

Time, the fourth dimension, perhaps humanity's most important concept.

Do we make the most of our time or, more accurately put, how do we make the most of our time?

We measure most things in what we get done and what we don't get done.

In any case, we blame it on time when we're dissatisfied, it's always time which is to blame, as if it's responsible for our inability to organize ourselves better.

Regardless of priority, there's always something which remains undone, something we would have liked to have done - time again.

We say we don't have time for this or that. The question of priority has a different meaning for each of us.

Poor old time, does it ever have a bad conscience?

My view of time is that I see it in relation to eternity, only ideally speaking, of course. I am probably quite realistic as regards to my own physical life here on earth, but I still like to see time from a "perspective of eternity".

Is it something to do with the fact that things live on? In that case, in which way and through what or whom, is not really of great significance. The most important for me is the belief that things live on.

History proves that things live on. I don't mean things I guess, they disappear, but time? History doesn't exist without time.

If something lasts forever it must be time and nothing but time.

Everything is regulated according to time. Absolutely everything. I can't think of a single thing which, in one form or other, isn't related to time.

Our time of birth is for astrologers crucial and determinate both for the way we are and for the way we develop. Here it hasn't got to do with just the day, the hour and the minute are also of the utmost significance.

Time is of the essence.

It was in the past that you had plenty of time. Was it perhaps less important to be on time for everything in those days, or did you have more time as, for instance, timetables weren't as developed as they are today?

Do opportunities create the rush for time?

With all the alternatives to be found for everything, it seems to be in the nature of things to have so much to be on time for.

Or is it the rush for time which creates the opportunities? What came first, the rush for time or the opportunities? Probably a balanced development.

Do we control time, or does it control us?

We compete in milliseconds - without time, no winners, and if there are no winners there are also no losers.

Does that mean that we can blame time for having losers? Someone must take the blame; everything becomes much easier then.

"Timing", it is said, is an important factor in all things. It means that the time aspect must be correct.

Despite all the analysis in the world, correct "timing" is difficult, if not impossible to calculate.

History repeats itself; it is said - rightly or wrongly. I don't know, but in my opinion, there is never a repetition, precisely because of time.

When the repetition takes place at a different time, it can't be the same which is being repeated. That makes me happy.

It's also good that we don't know too much about the future.

Time must be the greatest invention in the world.

MY FOOD FOR THOUGHT ON TIME

TIME I

It's not so important what Time it is - what's important is that it passes.

TIME II

If there is something that lasts forever it must be Time and nothing but the time.

2018

TIME MUST TAKE THE BLAME

We measure most things in what we get done and what we don't get done. In any case, we Blame it on Time when we are dissatisfied. It's always Time which is to Blame - as if it's responsible for our inability to organize ourselves better.

2015

TIME III

We compete in milliseconds - without Time,
no winners and no losers.

April 1994

WE ARE ALL DIFFERENT

Jan. 2017

Only when we admit that we are different and are willing to take that debate, are we capable of forming a just and workable democracy.

Of course, it's more popular, to say that we are alike, there's more solidarity and security in it.

That democracy implies that we are alike in relation to law and regulations, is both obvious and just, and that we are equipped with the same number of legs, arms, ears, and eyes, situated the same place on our body, are clear equality features.

That we come in two different issues in form of female and male, we luckily take for granted.

When I claim that we humans aren't alike, I don't talk about groups, colour of skin, religious beliefs, and such.

We all have our complete and unique identity. Whether it's about DNA, fingerprint, or other forms of identification, none of us on the entire planet are alike.

Shouldn't that give a good explanation of why expressions like: "we are all alike", are not only wrong, but totally misleading.

In my opinion, that is one of the most misguiding lies, we grow up with. Humans have never been and will never be alike.

Those predicting that we are alike, and that we are therefore expected to behave accordingly, are, in my opinion, completely on the wrong track.

If the Creator had meant that we should all be alike,

well, then he would never have equipped us with our unique individual identity.

The Creator didn't make this complicated curvature, to make us all unique, if he meant that we should all be alike.

The fact that we all are different is, of course, the reason why, in one or another form, we always compete. This goes for us all: we all compete, consciously or unconsciously.

If we were alike, the motive for competition would be lost, and the consequences of that would have been that we would have remained at the Stone Age level.

Why should we have been created as humans if it wasn't meant that we should develop? Wouldn't that have been totally meaningless? It's a fact that development only happens when competition is stimulated.

Whatever our faith, creation must have a meaning.

What I really want to emphasize is that the myth about us all being alike must get a total twist, for the world not to stop. We must turn the tide, and fully accept competition on all levels. If we do that, we at the same time accepts that we are basically different - and we are on the right track.

Realism must be cultivated and get a meaningful place in society; not as today where realism in many ways is looked upon as a bad word.

There is no form of racism in this, but a foundation for human survival.

Respect and tolerance must get a renewed importance and value. Values in general must be revised.

Reason suggests that a much too large part of the population is trapped by the dogma that we are alike, and so should be treated the same way. In my opinion it should go like this:

We are all different and unique and thus should be treated respectfully.

Our social system should function in a way that respects us as the different individuals we are and give us opportunities to develop individually.

We must not be forced into certain forms by rules and laws, which will turn out completely wrong and create great opposites. Changing attitudes must be voluntary.

Obviously, this require new thinking and greater demand must be made on society and business.

In all contexts, it is proven that everything depends on the leadership, and that this is the challenge.

Who should rule and decide is the question, and who should control that it happens within the rules, and in a transparent and just manner?

The concepts of justice must be made crystal clear and demand for fair leadership must be sharpened.

So far, democracy is – at least for us in the societies we belong to in the west –, the system giving the best compromise for just leadership.

In a democracy it is people, through their right of voting, who decide the political outcome - and that's the way it should be.

I never believed in the "enlightened one ruler system", even if it would be perfect if it would work in a just way.

However, the reason it doesn't work, and never will, is just because we are different.

The one who eventually should be the "enlightened one ruler" would be one of us, with the same strengths and weaknesses, meaning that the system could never work.

***

MY FOOD FOR THOUGHT ON
WE ARE ALL DIFFERENT

WE ARE ALL DIFFERENT

The reason why the "enlightened single ruler" system doesn't work, is because We Are All Different. As a consequence, the "enlightened single ruler" would be one of us with the same strengths and weaknesses.

2017

THE DIFFERENCE

We are not only created Different but between the extremes it's amazing how big the difference is.

Sept. 2019

DIFFERENCE I

Only when we admit that we are Different and willing to take that debate, are we capable of forming a just and viable democracy.

2018

DIFFERENT I

If the assertion that we are all Different is correct – and who can contradict that –,
being Different will be easier to accept and tolerate, as we are all in one form or another Different.